Extreme Mountain Biking

by Arlene Bourgeois Molzahn

Consultant:
Patrice Quintero
Communications Coordinator
National Off-Road Bicycle Association

CAPSTONE BOOKS

an imprint of Capstone Press
Mankato, Minnesota

Capstone Books are published by Capstone Press
151 Good Counsel Drive, P.O. Box 669, Mankato, Minnesota 56002
http://www.capstone-press.com

Library of Congress Cataloging-in-Publication Data
Molzahn, Arlene Bourgeois.
  Extreme mountain biking/by Arlene Bourgeois Molzahn.
  p.cm.—(Extreme sports)
  Includes bibliographical references and index.
  Summary: Describes the history of mountain bike racing and the equipment,
skills, techniques, and safety concerns involved in this competitive sport.
  ISBN 0-7368-0483-8
  1. All terrain cycling—Juvenile literature. 2. Extreme sports—Juvenile literature.
[1. All terrain cycling.] I. Title. II. Series.
GV1056.M65 2000
796.6'3—dc21   99-049276

Editorial Credits
Angela Kaelberer, editor; Timothy Halldin, cover designer; Kia Bielke, production
  designer and illustrator; Heidi Schoof, photo researcher

Photo Credits
Bicycle Museum of America, 10
Dugald Bremner Studio/Dugald Bremner, 16
Frank S. Balthis, 7
International Stock, 15
Larry Prosor, cover, 18, 21, 26, 31, 46
Mercury Press/Isaac Hernández, 4, 24–25, 28, 32, 39, 41; David Gala, 37
Photo Network/Brooks Dodge, 22
Uniphoto, Bruce Waters, 12
USA Cycling, 8

1 2 3 4 5 6 05 04 03 02 01 00

Table of Contents

Chapter 1   Extreme Mountain Biking 5

Chapter 2   History 11

Chapter 3   Equipment and Safety 17

Chapter 4   Skills 27

Chapter 5   Competition 33

Features

Photo Diagram 24

Words to Know 42

To Learn More 44

Useful Addresses 45

Internet Sites 47

Index 48

Chapter 1
Extreme Mountain Biking

Extreme mountain biking is a sport in which people race mountain bikes. They race over rough mountain terrain such as dirt trails and rocky mountainsides. Mountain bikes sometimes are called all-terrain bikes. These bicycles have special features that allow cyclists to ride them off paved roads.

Many mountain bicyclists compete in mountain bike races. Some of these cyclists are amateur racers. These racers compete mostly for fun. Other cyclists are professional

Many cyclists compete in mountain bike races.

racers. These racers compete in races to win prize money. They compete in many races during the racing season. Professional racers often do not have jobs outside of mountain bike racing.

Bike Races

Extreme mountain bike racers can compete in several types of races. These include cross-country, dual slalom, hillclimb, downhill, and endurance races.

Cross-country races take place on dirt roads and trails filled with obstacles. These may include brush, tree branches, bumps, boulders, slippery rocks, and mudholes. Cross-country races usually include four to six laps of the trail. One lap usually equals about 5 miles (8 kilometers). Racers ride in a group. The first racer to cross the finish line is the winner.

In dual slalom races, two cyclists race against each other. They race on side-by-side downhill courses. These courses are similar to slalom ski race courses. The courses have many twists and turns. Thin poles with flags

Cross-country mountain bike racers ride in a group.

mark these turns. These poles are called gates. Racers are penalized if they miss any turns. Race officials add time to their finish time. The racers then switch courses for a second race. The racers' times from the two races are combined. The racer with the fastest combined time is the winner.

Hillclimbs are slower than other races. These races test a racer's strength and

endurance on a trail filled with obstacles. Racers may either ride up the trail one by one or in a group. The winner reaches the top of the course in the shortest amount of time.

Downhill races begin on mountaintops. Racers ride one by one down a marked trail to a set finish point. The racers must avoid obstacles on the trail. The racer with the fastest riding time is the winner.

Endurance races are the longest of all extreme mountain bike races. These races can cover several hundred miles or kilometers. They can last as long as a week. Endurance racers usually travel both day and night to complete races. The first racer to cross the finish line wins the race.

Downhill racers ride one by one down a marked trail.

Chapter 2
History

In 1817, a German man named Baron Karl von Drais invented the first bicycle. This wooden bicycle had two wheels, handlebars, and a seat. But it had no pedals. Riders started and stopped the bicycle by placing their feet on the ground.

In 1839, a Scottish man named Kirkpatrick Macmillan invented a bicycle with pedals. This bicycle was called a velocipede.

A metal bicycle called an ordinary was popular in the 1870s and 1880s. An English man named James Starley invented this bicycle in 1871. The ordinary had a large front wheel

The first bicycles were made of wood.

Cyclists race BMX bikes on motocross courses.

and a much smaller back wheel. The rider sat high above the large front wheel.

By the 1890s, bicycles with brakes and rubber tires were common. These bicycles were called safety bicycles. They had two wheels of equal size. The bicycles also had one gear attached to the pedals to power the back wheel. This gear consisted of a metal chain and a toothlike wheel called a sprocket. The gear made the bicycle easier to steer and ride.

In 1895, a man named Jean Loubeyre invented the derailleur (di-RAY-luhr). This device allowed cyclists to shift the position of the chain to different sprockets as they rode. By the 1930s, manufacturers made bicycles that had more than one gear. The most common of these bicycles was the 10-speed. This bicycle had 10 gears. Cyclists used some gears to travel on flat, smooth land. They used others to climb up or ride down hills.

BMX and Mountain Bikes

In the 1970s, bicycle manufacturers made the first BMX bikes. BMX stands for "bicycle motocross." BMX bikes have small, sturdy metal frames and wide tires. Cyclists use these bikes to race on motocross courses. These dirt courses have many dirt mounds. BMX cyclists jump their bikes over these mounds.

People saw BMX cyclists ride their bikes off roads. Some of these people wanted bikes that could ride over mountain trails and other rough terrain. But BMX bikes have only one gear.

Cyclists cannot adjust gears on these bikes to allow for different riding conditions. Bicycles such as 10-speeds had several gears. But they were not strong enough to handle rough off-road riding.

Some cyclists changed their 10-speed bikes to make them more like BMX bikes. These modified bicycles had stronger frames and knobbies. These fat tires have wide treads with raised rubber bumps. The bumps give the tires a great deal of traction. This keeps the bicycles from slipping on rough trails.

At first, cyclists called the new bikes "clunkers." By the 1980s, people called them "all-terrain bikes" or "mountain bikes." Bicycle companies soon manufactured and sold mountain bikes.

Mountain Bike Racing

Mountain bike racing began in the 1980s in California. Groups of mountain bicyclists raced up and down mountain trails.

In 1983, several mountain bicyclists formed the National Off-Road Bicycle Association

Mountain bike racing began in the 1980s in California.

(NORBA). This group developed rules for mountain bike races. It also organized the first official races.

Extreme mountain biking became a popular sport in the late 1980s. The number of races has increased greatly since then. Today, NORBA sanctions about 1,000 races each year. These races meet NORBA's rules and guidelines.

Chapter 3
Equipment and Safety

A good mountain bike is an extreme mountain bike racer's most important piece of equipment. But mountain bike racers also rely on other types of equipment to win races and stay safe.

Mountain Bike Frames

Extreme mountain bicyclists need fast, sturdy mountain bikes. Cyclists ride their bikes over many obstacles. Their bikes must be strong and durable. They must last for a long time.

Mountain bikes must also be lightweight. Cyclists must carry their bikes in places where they cannot ride them. Cyclists also use less

Extreme mountain bicyclists need sturdy mountain bikes.

Most mountain bike frames are made of aluminum or titanium.

energy riding a lightweight bike. This is important during a race or on a long ride.

Mountain bike manufacturers continue to improve mountain bikes. They make bikes that are faster and stronger. The first mountain bikes only had five gears. Today, most mountain bikes have 15 to 24 gears. This variety of gears helps racers ride on different road conditions while maintaining their speeds.

The first mountain bikes were made of steel. These frames were strong but heavy. Today, most mountain bike frames are made of aluminum or titanium. Both of these metals are lightweight and strong. Titanium frames are stronger than aluminum frames. But titanium frames are more expensive. Most extreme mountain bike racers ride bikes with titanium frames.

Accessories and Clothing

Manufacturers make many types of clothing and accessories for mountain cyclists. This clothing and equipment is designed to keep cyclists comfortable and safe.

A helmet is a cyclist's most important accessory. A helmet can prevent a serious head injury from a fall. Most bicycle helmets are made of hard plastic and foam. They usually have a removable pad to improve their fit on the cyclist's head. Some helmets cover only the top of the head. Others cover the top and the sides of the head and parts of the face.

Professional mountain bike racers ride bikes with clipless pedals. These pedals have a locking mechanism. This device connects the racer's feet to the pedals. Clipless pedals allow racers to pull up on one pedal while pushing down on the other. This can increase racers' pedaling speeds as much as 40 percent.

Racers wear clipless bike shoes when riding bikes with clipless pedals. Clipless shoes have soles with specially designed cleats. These projecting pieces lock into the pedals.

Extreme mountain bike racers wear jerseys. These shirts are made of a lightweight material that draws sweat from the skin. This keeps the racer comfortable and helps prevent illnesses caused by changes in body temperature.

Racers often wear shorts with a synthetic fabric liner or pad in the crotch. The liners help prevent discomfort or sores. This is important during long endurance races.

Most racers wear cycling gloves. These gloves have padded palms to absorb the shock from the handlebars while riding over rough terrain. The padding helps prevent racers' hands, wrists, and arms from becoming tired. Most cycling gloves do not have fingers. This gives racers a better grip on the handlebars. But

Most racers wear cycling gloves and sports glasses.

downhill racers wear gloves with fingers.
Downhill racers crash more often than other
racers. The gloves protect their hands during
a crash.

Racers usually wear sports glasses to protect
their eyes from sun, insects, branches, mud, and
dust. Many racers carry lenses with different
tints that slip into the glasses' frames. They put
darker lenses in on sunny days. They wear lighter
lenses on cloudy days or when riding at night.

Racers should check their bikes carefully before each race or long ride.

Cyclists who ride in cold weather usually wear arm warmers, knee warmers, and leg warmers. These accessories look like sleeves with both ends open. This allows cyclists to easily slip them on and off.

Safety Equipment
Extreme mountain bike racers use their skills to win races. But they also keep safety in mind.

Racers want to stay free from injuries. A serious injury can end a racer's career.

All cyclists should carry some basic safety equipment. Identification, a small tool kit, and a first-aid kit prepare cyclists for emergencies. Cyclists should also carry a water bottle, sunscreen, insect repellent, and sunglasses.

Racers should carry some coins in case they need to use a pay phone to call for help. Many extreme mountain bike racers also carry cellular phones on long races. Racers can use these phones to call for help in case of an emergency. But these phones do not always work in remote areas. Cyclists should never ride alone in remote areas.

Safety Steps

Extreme mountain bike racers should check their bikes for wear or damage before every race or long ride. They should check the brakes, derailleurs, handlebars, wheels, chain, and tire pressure. Racers also should clean and inspect their bikes after every race or long ride.

Top extreme mountain cyclists keep safety in mind as they train. Training and riding safely can mean the difference between a short racing career and a long one.

Knobby

Chain

Derailleur

Brake Cable

Brake Lever

Gear Shift

Gears

Clipless Pedals

Chapter 4
Skills

Extreme mountain bike racers need several abilities in order to be successful. These include strength, endurance, and balance. Racers also learn special technical skills and stunts that help them avoid obstacles during races. Racers train many hours each day to develop these abilities and skills.

Training and Cross-Training

Most mountain bike races are in the summer. Racers mainly train in the winter. During winter, racers ride for several hours every day on level trails. They work to build up their balance,

Mountain bike racers learn special stunts to help them avoid obstacles.

3 miles (4.8 kilometers) faster per hour than a racer riding alone. Drafting does not work on hilly or mountainous terrain. This is because riding uphill does not create enough air resistance.

Extreme Stunts

Extreme mountain cyclists have developed several stunts. These technical feats help them avoid obstacles on trails.

Cyclists sometimes perform bunny hops. They crouch down on the bike. They then stand up and pull the bike up with them. This lifts both wheels off the ground. Cyclists often use this move to jump over trail obstacles or street curbs.

Cyclists also use wheelies to clear obstacles. Wheelies are similar to bunny hops. But cyclists keep pedaling with one wheel in the air when performing wheelies. Cyclists can lift either wheel off the ground when performing wheelies. It is much more difficult to lift the back wheel off the ground.

Cyclists perform some stunts just for fun. These stunts include table-tops and tweaks.

It is difficult to perform a wheelie with the back wheel off the ground.

Cyclists perform table-tops by jumping over an obstacle and twisting the bike sideways while they are in mid-air. Cyclists perform tweaks by twisting their handlebars back and forth in mid-air during a jump.

   These stunts are difficult and can be dangerous. Experienced cyclists practice for a long time to master these stunts.

Chapter 5
Competition

Extreme mountain bike racers can compete in different classes of races. Racers are separated into different classes according to age and ability.

Racers receive points for each race they compete in. The number of points depends on how high they place in the race. These points help determine which racers advance to national and world championship races.

Racing Classes
Mountain bike racers are divided into four classes. Inexperienced racers compete in the beginner class. Racers advance to two

Mountain bike racers compete in different types of races.

semi-professional classes as they gain experience and win races. These are the sport and expert classes. Intermediate cyclists compete in the sport class. Advanced cyclists compete in the expert class.

The pro or elite class is for professional cyclists. Each year, professional cyclists in the United States must receive a license. This document allows racers to enter the more difficult or well-known races. U.S. racers receive licenses from an organization such as the National Off-Road Bicycle Association (NORBA). In Canada, the Canadian Cycling Association (CCA) issues racing licenses.

Racers sometimes are separated by age as well as by ability. Racers ages 19 to 23 compete in the junior class. The espoir class is for men age 19 to 23. The senior class is open to racers ages 19 to 29. The masters class is for racers age 30 and older. Some racers fit into more than one class. For example, a 27-year-old beginning racer would be a senior beginner. But age categories do not apply to professional racers. They can race in the professional class as long as they are able.

Mountain Biking Slang

bail—to jump off a bike in order to avoid a crash

brain bucket—a helmet

cashed—too tired to ride any farther

chunder—to crash

death cookies—baseball-size rocks on a trail

doubletrack—a trail wide enough for two bikes

endo—to be thrown over a bike's handlebars

gravity check—to fall off a bike

hammer—to ride fast and hard

potato chip—a bent wheel

singletrack—a trail wide enough for only one bike

steed—a mountain bike

yard sale—to crash and leave equipment scattered on the ground

Dictionary compiled by Jason Dulberg, Extreme Mountain Biking, http://extreme.nas.net. Reprinted with permission.

Racing Costs

A cyclist must pay a fee to compete in a race. The fee depends on the type of race.

Most professional mountain bike racers have sponsors. Sponsors usually are bicycle or bicycle equipment manufacturers. These companies help racers pay for entry fees, travel costs, and equipment. In return, racers use the companies' equipment or products during races. Some racers also promote the companies' equipment or products in TV commercials and magazine advertisements.

North American Races

Some races are open to both amateur and professional racers. These include the NORBA National Championship Series, the Sea Otter Classic, and the Canada Cup.

The NORBA National Championship Series takes place each spring through fall. It includes six races held at locations around the United States. Events include cross-country, dual slalom, hillclimb, and downhill races. Professional cyclists compete in this series to earn points toward their national rankings.

The Sea Otter Classic includes cross-country races.

The Sea Otter Classic takes place each March in Monterey, California. Both amateur and professional racers test their fitness and skills in the event's 12 races. These include downhill, dual slalom, and cross-country races.

The Canada Cup takes place each summer. This competition includes five races held at locations across Canada. Professional and amateur racers compete in events such as cross-country, downhill, and dual slalom races.

Professional Races

Some races are open only to professional mountain bike racers. These include the X-Games, the Iditasport, the World Cup Series, and the World Mountain Bike Championships.

In the mid-1990s, mountain bike races became part of the X-Games. The ESPN television network hosts this extreme sport competition each year. Different competitions are held for winter and summer sports. Today, mountain bike races no longer are part of the Summer X-Games. The Winter X-Games include only one mountain bike race.

The Iditasport is one of the most difficult endurance races. This 100-mile (161-kilometer) race takes place each February in Alaska. The race begins and ends at Big Lake Lodge near Anchorage. People may compete in the Iditasport on bicycles, snowshoes, or skis. Racers have 50 hours to complete this race.

The Iditasport Extreme is a longer version of the Iditasport. The race follows a 320-mile (515-kilometer) trail that winds through the Alaska Mountain Range. The trail begins in the town of Knik and ends in the town of McGrath.

The World Cup Series includes 16 races held in locations around the world.

Most racers need about a week to complete this race.

The World Cup Series begins in spring and ends in late summer. This competition includes eight downhill and eight cross-country races. These races take place in locations around the world.

The world's top mountain bike racers end their racing season with the World Mountain

Bike Championships. These championships include cross-country and downhill races in elite, espoir, and junior classes.

Olympic and Pan American Games

Cross-country mountain bike races are part of both the Olympic Games and the Pan American Games. The Olympic Games are held every four years during the summer. Athletes from around the world compete in sports such as track, swimming, and cycling during these games. The Pan American Games take place the summer before the Olympic Games. Athletes from Caribbean and North, South, and Central American countries compete in these games. The Pan American Games include most of the sports in the Olympic Games.

The top extreme mountain cyclists can earn a living from racing. But most cyclists compete because they enjoy the sport's physical and mental challenges. It takes a combination of skill, hard work, and luck to become a champion extreme mountain cyclist.

Cross-country mountain bike races are a part of the Olympic Games.

Words to Know

aluminum (uh-LOO-mi-nuhm)—a lightweight, silver-colored metal

derailleur (di-RAY-luhr)—a device that shifts gears on a bicycle

draft (DRAFT)—to follow closely behind another racer; extreme mountain bicyclists draft in order to increase their riding speeds.

endurance race (en-DUR-uhnss RAYSS)—a bicycle race that takes place over a difficult trail for a long period of time

knobby (NAH-bee)—a fat tire with wide treads and raised rubber bumps

obstacle (OB-stuh-kuhl)—an object that stands in a cyclist's way

slalom race (SLAH-luhm RAYSS)—a downhill bicycle race during which racers must ride through sets of gates

sponsor (SPON-sur)—a person or business that helps pay a racer's expenses

terrain (tuh-RAYN)—the surface of the land

titanium (tye-TAY-nee-uhm)—a strong, lightweight metal

traction (TRAK-shuhn)—the gripping power that keeps a bike from slipping on a surface

To Learn More

Armentrout, David. *Mountain Biking.* Sports Challenge. Vero Beach, Fla.: Rourke, 1997.

Glaser, Jason. *Snow Mountain Biking.* Extreme Sports. Mankato, Minn.: Capstone Books, 1999.

Gutman, Bill. *Mountain Biking.* Action Sports. Mankato, Minn.: Capstone Books, 1995.

Jensen, Julie. *Beginning Mountain Biking.* Beginning Sports. Minneapolis: Lerner Publications, 1997.

King, Andy. *Fundamental Mountain Biking.* Fundamental Sports. Minneapolis: Lerner Publications, 1997.

You can read articles about extreme mountain biking in *Bicycling Magazine* and *Mountain Bike Magazine.*

Useful Addresses

Adventure Cycling Association
P.O. Box 8308
Missoula, MT 59807

Canadian Cycling Association (CCA)
1600 James Naismith Drive
Suite 810
Gloucester, ON K1B 5N4
Canada

**International Mountain Bicycling
  Association (IMBA)**
P.O. Box 7578
Boulder, CO 80306

**National Off-Road Bicycle Association
  (NORBA)**
USA Cycling
One Olympic Plaza
Colorado Springs, CO 80909

Internet Sites

Adventure Cycling Association
http://www.adv-cycling.org

Canadian Cycling Association
http://www.canadian-cycling.com

Extreme Mountain Biking
http://extreme.nas.net

**International Mountain Bicycling
    Association**
http://www.greatoutdoors.com/imba

Mountain Biking Trail Sources
http://www.trailsource.com

**USA Cycling Online/National Off-Road
    Bicycle Association**
http://www.usacycling.org/mtb

Index

amateur racers, 5, 36–37

BMX bicycles, 13–14
brakes, 12, 23

Canada Cup, 36–37
cross-country races, 6,
    36–37, 39–40

derailleur, 13, 23
downhill races, 6, 9,
    36–37, 39–40
drafting, 29–30
dual slalom races, 6, 37

endurance races, 6, 9, 20,
    38

frame, 13–14, 19

gear, 12–13, 14, 18

hillclimb races, 6–7, 36

Iditasport, 38

license, 34

National Off-Road
    Bicycle Association
    (NORBA), 14–15, 34
NORBA National
    Championship Series,
    36

professional racers, 5–6,
    19, 34, 36–37, 38

racing classes, 33–34, 40

Sea Otter Classic, 36–37
skills, 22, 27, 37, 40
stunts, 27, 30–31

tires, 12, 13–14
training, 23, 27–29

World Cup Series, 38–39
World Mountain Bike
    Championships, 38–40

X-Games, 38

J
GV
1056
M65
2000

Molzahn, Arlene
  Bourgeois.

Extreme mountain
  biking.

$21.26

DATE DUE

OCT 24 2010

10-01